ALEXANDER THE GREAT

WORLD CONQUEROR

SPECIAL LIVES IN HISTORY THAT BECOME

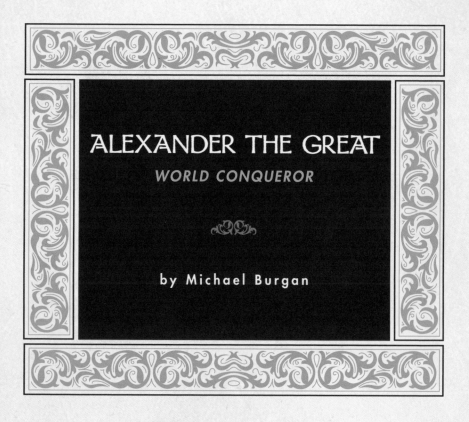

ALEXANDER THE GREAT
WORLD CONQUEROR

by Michael Burgan

*Content Adviser: Elizabeth Carney, Ph.D.,
History Professor, Clemson University*

*Reading Adviser: Susan Kesselring, M.A.,
Literacy Educator, Rosemount–Apple Valley–
Eagan [Minnesota] School District*

COMPASS POINT BOOKS ◈ MINNEAPOLIS, MINNESOTA

Compass Point Books
3109 West 50th Street, #115
Minneapolis, MN 55410

Visit Compass Point Books on the Internet at *www.compasspointbooks.com*
or e-mail your request to *custserv@compasspointbooks.com*

Editor: Anthony Wacholtz
Page Production: Noumenon Creative
Photo Researcher: Svetlana Zhurkin
Cartographer: XNR Productions, Inc.
Library Consultant: Kathleen Baxter

Art Director: Jaime Martens
Creative Director: Keith Griffin
Editorial Director: Carol Jones
Managing Editor: Catherine Neitge

Library of Congress Cataloging-in-Publication Data
Burgan, Michael
  Alexander the Great: World Conqueror / by Michael Burgan
      p. cm.—(Signature lives)
  Includes bibliographical references and index.
  ISBN-13: 978-0-7565-1872-1 (hardcover)
  ISBN-10: 0-7565-1872-5 (hardcover)
  1. Alexander, the Great, 356–323—Juvenile literature. 2. Generals—
Greece—Biography—Juvenile literature. 3. Greece—Kings and
rulers—Biography—Juvenile literature. 4. Greece—History—Macedonian
Expansion, 359–323 B.C.—Juvenile literature. I. Title. II. Series.
  DF234.B78 2007
  938'.07092—dc22   2006002993

ANCIENT GREECE

After the fall of Troy around 1180 B.C. in the Trojan War, soldiers returned to a Greece mired in famine and economic collapse. It was a time for rebuilding. Greece underwent a political and cultural transformation 400 years after the war with the transition to independent city-states and the establishment of the Olympics. Athens became the hub for developments in architecture, art, science, and philosophy. In about 460 B.C., ancient Greece entered its golden age, one that would produce the establishment of democracy, the beginnings of university study, great strides in medicine and science, architectural advancements, and the creation of plays and epic poems that are still enjoyed today.

Table of Contents

1 BATTLE FOR A KINGDOM

❧⟡❧

On a desert plain in Assyria in 331 B.C., two massive armies camped across from each other, waiting for battle. The undefeated army of Alexander III of Macedonia was preparing to attack the Persians, led by their "Great King," Darius III.

Alexander commanded one of the most fearsome armies the world had ever known. He launched an invasion of Asia to pay back the Persians for their attack on Greece almost 150 years earlier. The invasion, he hoped, would also bring him wealth and glory. Alexander had shown great skill as a commander, able to win the trust of his men. Alexander also had unlimited self-confidence, fueled by his belief that he was the descendant of ancient Greek heroes and was blessed by the gods.

Alexander led his troops into battle atop his trusted horse, Bucephalas.

In two years of fighting, Alexander had already captured Asia Minor, Egypt, and other lands under Persian control. Now he was approaching the heart of Persia itself. The war against Darius was no longer just about getting revenge for past Persian wrongs against the Macedonians and Greeks. Alexander wanted to capture and control the whole Persian Empire. His march east brought him to the small Assyrian town of Gaugamela, in what is now northern Iraq. There, in September 331, Darius had set up his camp to wait for Alexander's advance. As his men huddled around bonfires, Darius walked with a torch to inspect his troops, concerned about the upcoming battle. Never before had Darius led such a powerful force. But he knew he would need these great numbers if he hoped to defeat Alexander.

Toward the end of the month, Earth cast its shadow over a full moon, darkening the evening sky. This lunar eclipse frightened some of Alexander's troops, who saw it as a bad omen. But Alexander's seer, Aristander, assured the young commander that the eclipse was a good sign. The two armies would clash before the end of the month, Aristander said, and Alexander's Macedonian army would win.

As the time for battle drew near, Alexander inspired his troops as he had before past victories. One historian described the situation:

[The troops] were to urge each man in the moment of danger to attend in his own place in the line to the requirements of order, to keep perfect silence when that was necessary in the advance, and by contrast to give a ringing shout when it was right to shout, and a howl to inspire the greatest terror when the moment came to howl.

Some of Alexander's officers, however, did not share the seer's faith in a victory. One night, Alexander's most experienced general, Parmenion, came to the king's tent. He told Alexander that the Macedonians might be better off attacking the Persians at night, under the cover of darkness. Alexander knew from history that night battles posed certain dangers. Forces could lose their sense of

Alexander consulted his seer, Aristander, at the altar fire before the battle of Gaugamela.

direction and attack their own troops. And once the enemy knew they were under attack, the darkness could help them escape or counterattack. But Alexander had another reason to oppose a surprise attack at night: his pride. He told Parmenion, "I will not [dishonor] myself by stealing victory like a thief." He would defeat Darius in an open and honest fight.

In the last days of September, Alexander inched his troops closer to Darius' camp. The Macedonians and Greeks were vastly outnumbered. Darius had about 34,000 cavalry and 200,000 infantry, or foot soldiers, under his command. Alexander led only about 7,000 cavalry and 40,000 infantry. But earlier victories against the Persians—and the seer's prediction—boosted Alexander's confidence. Finally, on October 1, the great battle began, and as the seer

Alexander's army clashed with the forces of Darius at Gaugamela.

had said, Alexander triumphed.

Alexander had won the greatest victory of his life and one of the most important battles ever fought in world history. Alexander gained control of the Persian Empire as he had dreamed, but he was not done fighting. He pushed beyond the eastern boundary of Persia into India, hoping to expand his empire. Finally, in 326, the exhausted Macedonian troops rebelled against their commander. Tired of war, they missed their families and wanted to go home. Alexander agreed.

Alexander never spent much time ruling his homeland. He spent his adult life as a soldier on the battlefield. But his victories led to the creation of Greek Macedonian kingdoms in Asia and Africa. He also founded new cities and populated them with Macedonians and Greeks. Their language and culture spread far beyond the Greek homelands, and their influence lasted for centuries. Tales of Alexander's deeds are still told in the distant lands he conquered. Thanks to his success in war and powerful effect on world history, the young Macedonian king is known as Alexander the Great.

Details of Alexander's battles are not always complete. The ancient biographies of Alexander were written hundreds of years after he lived by people who saw only fragments of the original sources. The writers often tried to make Alexander look better—or worse—than he really was. To understand Alexander and his times, modern historians must sift through all the ancient histories—most of which are more than 2,000 years old—and decide what is true.

2 DESTINED FOR GREATNESS

❧⟨⟩❧

Alexander's family had no doubts that he would rise to greatness. Both his father, King Philip II, and his mother, Queen Olympias, came from royal families. According to legends that Alexander believed, his father's family traced its roots back to Heracles, an ancient Greek hero. Heracles, also known as Hercules, was famous for his great strength. The Greeks considered Hercules a demi-god—half human and half god. His father was said to have been Zeus, the most powerful of the many gods the Greeks worshipped. Legends also said that on his mother's side, Alexander descended from Achilles, another Greek hero and demi-god. Courage and strength were part of Alexander's family history, and they flowed through him as well.

Alexander's father, Philip II, became king of Macedonia in 359 B.C. at the age of 21.

Stories were told to suggest the greatness Alexander would show. When his mother was pregnant with him, she dreamed that she heard the roar of thunder and saw a bolt of lightning strike her womb. The bolt sparked a fire that spread into the distance. The baby that Olympias carried, her dream suggested, would have the same dazzling—and destructive—impact as the lightning and its fire. Earlier, Philip had dreamed that he sealed shut his wife's womb, and on the seal was the image of a lion. The seer Aristander said the dream meant Olympias would have a son with a lion's ferocity and courage.

On the day Alexander was born—most likely July 20, 356 B.C.— more signs seemed to point to his future accomplishments. On the battlefield, Philip captured the city of Potidaea. At the same time, his general Parmenion was winning another important battle. And at Olympia, the site of the original Olympic Games, Philip's horse won a race. According to the ancient historian Plutarch, Philip's seers told him that "the son, whose birth coincided with three victories would himself prove invincible."

When Alexander was born, Philip was fighting to unite all of Greece under his control. He had already enlarged Macedonia through conquest and now wanted more. At the time, the Greeks were not united into one government. In southern Greece there were a number of city-states, and in northern Greece there were some

Alexander's mother, Olympias (c. 375-316 B.C.)

kingdoms. Greek influence extended to Asia Minor as well, where the Greeks had also founded cities. In the fifth century B.C., Athens had become the dominant city in Greece. It was also a center of art and learning. A war with the rival city of Sparta, however, left Athens weakened. Through the first decades of the fourth century B.C., Athens, Sparta, and several other Greek cities competed for dominance. Meanwhile, to their north, the kingdom of Macedonia was growing.

The Macedonian royal family considered itself Greek, even though they were far from the primary city-states. Centuries before, the Greeks had set up colonies along Macedonia's Aegean coast, and the

Ancient Greece, around 400 B.C.
Present-day Greece boundary

Black Sea

Thrace

Macedonia

Illyria

Pella
Mieza
Amphipolis
Stagirus
Eion
Thasos

Mt. Olympus
Potidaea

Epirus

Hellespont River
(Dardanelles)

Thessaly

Assus

Phrygia

Aegean

Mytilene

Lesbos

ASIA MINOR

Mt. Parnassus
Delphi
Plataea
Thebes
Euboea
Sea
Gulf of Corinth
Corinth
Attica
Marathon
Athens
Olympia
Argos

Peloponnesus

Sparta

Delos
Naxos

Miletus
Halicarnassus

Cos

Melos

Rhodes

N
W E
S

0   90 miles
0   90 kilometers

Crete

Mediterranean Sea

Ancient Greeks lived in places outside of the boundaries of modern-day Greece.

people spoke a form of Greek. The citizens of the city-states, however, considered the Macedonians backward country folk, not true Greeks. Macedonia had only a few cities and lacked a tradition of democracy, which the Athenians saw as the best possible form of government. But Macedonia did have natural resources, such as timber, grain, and pastures for grazing sheep. And with Philip's first conquests, Macedonia took control of gold and silver mines that yielded great wealth. Using his new fortunes, Philip built a well-trained, professional army and funded his plan for conquest. With each victory, he gained more wealth and power.

As the son of a king, Alexander had a comfortable childhood. He and his sister Cleopatra grew up in the Macedonian capital of Pella. Young Greek boys of that time learned to hunt and play sports. Alexander was a fast runner, and friends once asked if he wanted to compete at the Olympic Games. He said he would, but only if he could run against kings. Mere athletes were not good enough competition for him.

Philip wanted to make sure Alexander developed his mind as well as his body, and the young prince had a number of teachers. The most famous was Aristotle, a great Greek philosopher. In his many writings, Aristotle explored all parts of human experience: art, politics, science, and ethics—the study of the nature of good and bad behavior. Aristotle taught Alexander and several other students outdoors, at a place near Pella called Mieza.

As a boy, Alexander learned about the stories of Homer, a Greek poet said to have written *The Iliad*. Aristotle then gave the young prince a better grasp of the story's meaning. *The Iliad* detailed the Greek war against the city of Troy, in Asia Minor, hundreds

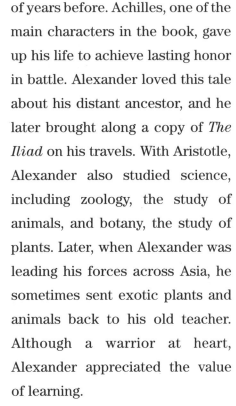

of years before. Achilles, one of the main characters in the book, gave up his life to achieve lasting honor in battle. Alexander loved this tale about his distant ancestor, and he later brought along a copy of *The Iliad* on his travels. With Aristotle, Alexander also studied science, including zoology, the study of animals, and botany, the study of plants. Later, when Alexander was leading his forces across Asia, he sometimes sent exotic plants and animals back to his old teacher. Although a warrior at heart, Alexander appreciated the value of learning.

As a boy, Alexander also showed an interest in religion. He followed the Greek tradition of honoring the gods by offering them burnt incense. His mother was deeply religious and belonged to some of the less traditional religious groups that flourished in Greece. She was said to take part in rituals that used live snakes. The rituals honored Dionysus, the god of wine and merriment. Olympias may have also told her son that Philip was not really his father and that, instead, he was the son of a god. Some Greeks believed this

King Philip's connection with Aristotle led to Alexander's education by the famous philosopher.

story, and Alexander later did, as well.

Olympias apparently wanted her son to think he was destined to do great things, an idea he eagerly accepted. At times, he resented his father's achievements on the battlefield. He told friends that because of his father, "there will be nothing great or spectacular for you and me to show the world." When he was about 13, Alexander showed a willingness to challenge his father, demonstrating a sharp mind and deep self-confidence.

One day, Alexander saw Philip and some of his friends watching a horse in the fields. The animal was called Bucephalas—Greek for "oxhead." The horse had a mark on his head that resembled an ox.

A man was offering to sell Bucephalas to the king for a high price. Philip, however, turned down the deal when he learned how wild the horse was. No one could mount the stallion, and he would not listen to commands. As Philip was about to send the horse seller away, Alexander spoke up. "What a horse they are losing," he said, "all because they don't know how to handle him."

At first, Philip ignored his son, but Alexander repeated his comments a few more times. Finally, the king said Alexander should not criticize people older and more experienced with horses than he was. Unless, of course, Alexander thought he could do better. The prince replied, "At least I could manage this one better." He promised to pay his father the price of the horse if he could not ride him. Philip and his friends laughed at the boy's challenge and accepted the bet.

Unlike the men, Alexander had noticed something about Bucephalas. The horse bucked and snorted the wildest when he saw his own shadow. Taking hold of the horse's reins, Alexander turned him toward the sun so he could not see his shadow. When Bucephalas calmed down, Alexander jumped on his back, and the horse sprinted off across the field. Stunned, the men first watched silently, then burst into applause. Philip now fully realized that his son had the skills to do great things. When Alexander returned, the king told him:

After taming Bucephalas, Alexander earned the respect of his father.

My boy, you must find a kingdom big enough for your ambitions. Macedonia is too small for you.

Philip bought Bucephalas from the horse seller and gave him to Alexander. In later years, the horse would be the young prince's constant companion in battle, and Alexander would fulfill his father's prediction of winning a large kingdom. ❧

LA COURSE

3 THRUST ONTO THE THRONE

汫z汫

Philip expected Alexander to one day join him on the battlefield. To prepare Alexander for life as a soldier, Philip entered him into the School of Royal Pages. He was one of about 50 boys who came from the best families in Macedonia. One of the other boys was Hephaestion, who became Alexander's closest friend and later one of his generals. Discipline at the school could be harsh. Philip served as the principal, and he beat students who disobeyed. From the age of 14 to the time they turned 18, the boys studied military affairs and improved their horse-riding skills. To build strength, they wrestled and did gymnastics. They also took classes, and it was during his time at the school that Alexander studied with Aristotle.

Although busy with his studies, Alexander also

had extra duties because of his father's position. One time when Philip was away at war, Alexander took his father's place and met with Persian officials visiting Pella. He asked intelligent questions while showing a friendly nature. The Persians, the historian Plutarch wrote, "were filled with admiration."

When Alexander was 16, his father gave him an even greater responsibility by naming him regent. In that position, Alexander served as the head of the government while Philip fought wars with the Greeks. According to customs of the time, Philip had several wives besides Olympias, and at least one of them had a son by Philip. Alexander, however, was clearly Philip's choice to rule Macedonia if he should die in battle. Alexander's new role brought extra prestige to Olympias, since being the mother of a king was a great honor.

While Alexander served as regent, a rebellion broke out in part of Macedonia. He led troops to put down the rebellion. To prevent further problems, he established a base for Macedonian troops in the defeated rebels' main city. Alexander also took Macedonians from other regions and resettled them there, creating a new city. It was called Alexandropolis—the first of many cities he would name after himself, imitating his father.

During this time, Philip angered Athenians by destroying ships that were bringing grain to their city. They convinced other nearby city-states to fight together against Macedonia. In 339, Alexander joined Philip on the battlefield. The next year, father and son led the Macedonians in their greatest battle in Greece. At Chaeronea, the Athenians and their allies had 35,000 infantry, which were called hoplites. Philip's forces included 30,000 infantry and 2,000 cavalry. The Greek and Macedonian infantry fought in a formation called a phalanx. The soldiers stayed close together in lines about eight soldiers deep. Alexander led some of the best cavalry troops.

Although slightly outnumbered, the Macedonians entered the battle with high spirits. They knew they were a well-trained and well-equipped army, while the Greeks were mostly part-time soldiers. And with Philip as their commander, the Macedonians had a general who had a proven knack for making the

The phalanx was introduced into Greek warfare centuries before Alexander became king.

Although history calls Alexander "the Great," his father built the army that Alexander used to win an empire. Philip perfected the sarissa, the main weapon used by his infantry. A sarissa was a long spear with a sharp tip at each end. It was much longer than the spear that Greek hoplites used, so the Macedonians could kill their opponents from a greater distance. With that advantage, the Macedonians did not need as much heavy armor, allowing their phalanxes to move more quickly in the field. Philip also improved siege engines, large weapons used to attack walled cities. He capped all his improvements by constantly training his men so they would have the strength and discipline to excel on the battlefield.

right decisions on the battlefield. Alexander soon showed that he could match his father's bravery and skill. According to the historian Diodorus of Sicily, Alexander "first succeeded in breaking the solid front of the enemy line and, striking down many, he fought those opposite him into the ground." Alexander and his men slaughtered the Sacred Band, 300 soldiers from the city of Thebes known for their courage. Elsewhere on the field, the Macedonian phalanxes used their long spears called sarissas to kill or wound thousands of enemy troops. When the battle ended, Philip was the undisputed ruler of Greece.

Philip did not take direct control of the defeated city-states. Instead, he organized them into a political organization called the Hellenic League, or League of Corinth. The league members had control of local affairs, but they pledged to fight for Philip when he asked them to. Given Philip's military strength,

Philip's Macedonian forces defeated the Athenians and Thebans at Chaeronea.

there was no question the league would accept all of his demands. With Philip's prodding, the league agreed to send Greek troops on a campaign against the Persian Empire.

Some Greeks had wanted to fight the Persians for years. In 490, Persia had attacked the Greek mainland. After a defeat, the Persians withdrew, but they returned 10 years later. This time, they destroyed Athens before the Greeks finally drove them off. The desire to avenge the Greek defeat in Athens 150 years earlier was the stated reason for going to war with Persia. But Philip was more interested in extending his power and increasing his wealth. In the spring of 336, combined Greek and Macedonian forces headed for Asia Minor.

As the league was forming and preparing for its war with the Persian Empire, Alexander was thrust into the middle of a family crisis. Philip gave a banquet to mark his marriage to another wife, a much younger Macedonian woman named Cleopatra, the same name as Alexander's sister. The bride's uncle, Attalus, gave a drunken toast praising the married couple. He hoped that Cleopatra would give Philip a son who would be the true heir to his father's kingdom. His comment suggested that someone related to Attalus would make a better king than Alexander.

The prince was insulted by the suggestion that he might not be good enough to rule one day as king. According to some historians, Alexander hurled a cup at Attalus. Philip rose to defend Attalus, who was also one of his generals. The king was drunk as well, and as he raised his sword and charged at Alexander, he fell. The prince supposedly said:

Around 550, the small kingdom of Persia, in modern Iran, began to expand. The Persians conquered the Medes, their neighbors to the north, and then took over the empire of Babylonia to the west. The Persians also won control of Greek cities in Africa and Asia Minor. Eventually, they governed lands stretching into modern Afghanistan and Pakistan. Cyrus the Great, the founder of the Persian Empire, split his new lands into regions called satrapies, ruled by a Persian official called a satrap. Within each satrapy, the local people had religious freedom and a large degree of control over their own affairs.

> *Here is the man who was making ready to cross from Europe to Asia, and who cannot even cross from one table to another without losing his balance.*

After this wedding-day spat, Olympias and Alexander left Pella. The queen was angry with Philip for threatening her son, and she returned to her homeland. Alexander spent time in Illyria, a northern region within Macedonia. Meanwhile, a friend of Philip advised the king to repair his relationship with Alexander. Father and son finally patched up their problems, and Alexander returned to Pella.

Another royal wedding led to even greater turmoil in Macedonia. In the summer of 336, Philip was ready to lead his main army into Asia Minor. Before he left, he arranged for the wedding of his daughter, Cleopatra, to a nearby king. The wedding was part of several days of feasts. As Philip entered a theater to attend a ceremony, one of his bodyguards rushed forward and stabbed him to death. Before the assassin could flee, several

Alexander and Olympias were both upset with Philip's actions at the wedding banquet.

other guards killed him.

The killer, Pausanias, had a grudge against Attalus and had asked Philip to punish him. Philip had refused, and so the angry and insulted Pausanias killed his king. The Macedonians believed that Pausanias had help carrying out his murder plot, and several other men were executed. The exact details of who may have been involved and why are not clear, and some people even whispered that Alexander and his mother played a role. Most modern historians

After ruling the Macedonian Empire for 23 years, Philip II was murdered.

reject this notion. Still, the queen and her son showed a ruthless streak in the days to come. Olympias had Philip's wife Cleopatra and her infant son killed, and Alexander ordered the killing of Attalus. The killings reflected the generally ruthless and violent nature of Macedonian politics.

Almost immediately after Philip's assassination, the Macedonian nobles met to choose a new king. These leading men of the kingdom gathered together in the theater, with Philip's dead body still in front of them. Some of Alexander's male relatives could make a claim to Philip's throne, and they had a few backers among the Macedonian nobles. But Alexander had the support of Antipater, one of the elder nobles and a friend of Philip's. When one of the nobles shouted, "Alexander, son of Philip," the rest agreed he should be king. At the age of 20, Alexander now ruled Macedonia and the surrounding Greek states. But he soon faced problems that threatened his position, and the Macedonian and Greek forces waited anxiously for Alexander to lead the invasion of Asia Minor. 🐾

4 FIRST SUCCESSES

‹੭✕੭ઝ୨

When the citizens of Athens heard about Philip's death, they rejoiced. Across the Hellenic League, people thought they would now regain their independence. But Alexander didn't want to lose his father's hard-earned empire. He tried to win support to rule Greece and to carry out Philip's planned war against the Persian Empire by talking with the Greeks. Helping him make his point was the Macedonian army, which marched with its king as he met with the Greeks. They were prepared to act if Alexander's words did not convince the Greeks.

Parts of Greece, however, rejected Alexander's rule, and citizens of Illyria and Thrace rebelled. In 335 B.C., with a force of about 25,000 infantry and 5,000 cavalry, Alexander squashed the rebellions.

Greek and Macedonian infantry marched in a phalanx behind Alexander.

As the fighting came to an end in Illyria, Alexander learned that a rebellion was underway in Thebes. He quickly moved his forces south—so quickly that the other Greek city-states didn't have time to send aid to Thebes. At first, Alexander waited outside the city, saying he only wanted the men who had spurred the revolt. When the Thebans refused to turn them over, he launched a devastating attack. After some fighting outside the city, the Macedonians stormed the walls. During the battle, 6,000 Thebans were killed. Another 30,000 were captured and sold into slavery, and Alexander had the city razed. He hoped his brutal treatment of the Thebans would convince other Greeks not to challenge his rule. Yet Alexander did spare the lives of some Thebans, including people who had opposed the rebellion, priests, and relatives of Pindar, one of Alexander's favorite poets.

With Thebes crushed, Alexander could finally turn his focus to the campaign against the Persian Empire. Before he left, he looked to the gods for help. At Delphi, he visited the oracle, a religious site where gods were believed to speak to specially chosen priests, also called oracles. The oracle priestess told Alexander it was not a good day to receive the gods' words, but Alexander persisted. Finally, the oracle told him, "You are invincible, my son!" Alexander left happy, hearing the words he wanted to hear. He also visited Macedonia before he left, where he held

Alexander often followed the advice of oracles, especially the oracle at Delphi.

religious ceremonies in honor of Zeus. Finally, in the spring of 334, Alexander was ready to fight again.

By the time he was 22, Alexander was the unchallenged ruler of Greece and a successful general. Although he was fairly short, his body was muscular. Some observers commented on his fair skin and said that his face turned red easily. The Roman historian Aelian wrote that Alexander was considered good-looking, with light, curly hair. But he also noted that "there was something in his appearance that aroused fear."

Alexander believed he was part of a long tradition of Greek heroes. Soon after landing in Asia Minor, he visited the city of Troy. There, he went to the grave of Achilles, his ancestor who had once fought so bravely for the Greeks against Troy. Alexander also made a sacrifice to Athena, the goddess of war. At the temple of Athena, he took a shield and weapons that Greeks had left there in her honor. Later during his Asian campaign, Alexander would be wounded in battle and carried off the field on the shield he had taken.

Even more threatening to Alexander's foes was the army he led. He now commanded a force of 32,000 infantry and 5,000 cavalry. The army included some of the best Macedonian fighters, as well as soldiers from the Greek city-states. Alexander led them to the Hellespont, a narrow stretch of water that separated Europe and Asia. The army sailed across the river and linked up with the forces Philip had sent ahead before he died. Some sources claim Alexander was the first one to come ashore in Asia. As he landed, he said, "I accept from the gods Asia won by the spear." The king had no doubt that he would defeat the Persians.

Meanwhile, the Persians tried to prepare for the enemy's attack. Memnon, a Greek mercenary, commanded the Persian troops in the region. He advised burning the countryside to deprive Alexander of the grain needed to feed his troops. The satrap of this part of the empire, however, disagreed. He did not want to destroy his own lands, and he believed the Persians should challenge Alexander. Under

Memnon, the Persians had pushed back the first Macedonian troops sent by Philip, and they hoped for the same success against Alexander.

In May 334, the Persians massed 40,000 troops, half of them cavalry, along the east side of the Granicus River in what is now eastern Turkey. Alexander approached with all of his cavalry and just under half of his ground troops. As he reached the west bank of the river, he saw the enemy waiting for him. His

Alexander prepared to cross the Granicus River at the head of the cavalry.

general Parmenion suggested they wait until early the next morning to cross the river. Alexander rejected the idea—he wanted to fight right away and show the Persians his courage. He said he did not want the Persians "to think they were as good as soldiers as we are."

For a moment, a hush fell over the riverbank. Then battle trumpets blared, and the Macedonians shouted "Engalius," the name of an ancient Greek war god. Alexander's forces formed a line more than 2 miles (3.2 kilometers) long. Part of the army headed for the center of the Persian cavalry waiting on the other shore. As the fighting began, Alexander rode his beloved horse Bucephalas across the Granicus. A white feather on his helmet indicated he was the commander. His men would always know where he was on the battlefield and see his bravery. But the Persians could spot him easily, too, and they tried their best to kill him. Alexander went through several spears during the fighting, and an enemy's sword hacked off part of his helmet. Before the Persian could swing again at the stunned king, Cleitus, one of Alexander's commanders, stepped in. He speared the Persian, saving Alexander's life.

In and along the river, the two sides fought hand-to-hand. But once again, the superior weapons of the Macedonians, their sarissas, helped them to defeat the Persians. Once ashore, the Macedonians

Alexander's cavalry emerged from the Granicus River, slaughtering the Persian infantry.

slaughtered most of the Greek mercenaries who had not had time to enter the battle. The rest were sent back to Greece as slaves. Several thousand Persians died, while Alexander lost only about 100 men. After the battle, Alexander visited some of his wounded troops and buried the enemy's dead. He also sent back to Athens 300 suits of Persian armor to tell the Greeks of his victory. Along with the armor was a message: "Alexander, son of Philip, and the Greeks ... dedicate these spoils, taken from the Persians who dwell in Asia." The Greeks would know that their defeat in Athens 150 years earlier had been avenged. Alexander wanted the Greeks to believe that he fought for them and not just for his own glory.

The Macedonian army now headed south to Sardis. The Persian commander surrendered the city without a fight. From there, Alexander traveled along the eastern coast of the Aegean Sea, taking control of several cities with large Greek populations. Alexander let the citizens form democratic governments to run local affairs. Alexander was not in favor of democracy, but he wanted to keep the Greeks happy as he continued his conquest of Persia. He showed mercy to citizens who had been forced to fight against the Macedonians. Although sometimes bloodthirsty on the field, Alexander showed great political skill. His thoughtful treatment of these local people won their support.

Despite the losses it suffered, Persia still had a powerful navy. A fleet of about 400 ships was just about to enter the Aegean Sea. Alexander knew his naval forces were not as strong. Still, Parmenion

As he conquered, Alexander left trusted people in charge of his new lands. Ada, the former queen of a region called Caria, won Alexander's trust when she helped arrange the surrender of a Carian city to the Macedonians. He then named her governor of Caria. Ada became the only woman ever given such a high post by the Greeks or Macedonians during wartime. Ada and Alexander had a close personal relationship, as well. She sent him gifts, including candy, and adopted him as her son.

advised that the Greek fleet should attack the Persian ships. Alexander disagreed. He had seen what he believed to be an omen: an eagle, a bird associated with Zeus. Since the eagle was on land, Alexander believed the omen directed him to attack the Persian navy on land, not at sea. This meant capturing the ports the Persians used for their ships. He decided to send most of his ships back to Greece so he would not have to spend money on them and their sailors. Some modern historians think this was one of Alexander's few military blunders. He later had to create a new fleet to face a Persian naval threat in the Aegean Sea.

Alexander's first battle under his new strategy came at the coastal city of Miletus. Using siege engines, his forces knocked down the city's walls. Next, he advanced on Halicarnassus. The defense there was tougher, and although the Macedonians

Siege engines were effective for breaking down the walls of an enemy's fortress.

took control of most of the city, some Persian forces remained there for several years. Alexander and his men then headed east along the coast of the Mediterranean Sea before turning north into a region called Phrygia. Alexander had already sent a force under Parmenion to take control there.

In 333, the Macedonian armies and their reinforcements met in Gordium, the capital of Phrygia. Alexander took time from warfare to address an old and challenging puzzle. Gordium was known for a famous knot tied in wood. The Gordian knot held together a wagon and a yoke. Legends said that whoever untied the knot and separated the wagon from the yoke would rule Asia. No one, however, had ever come close to undoing the knot. According to some sources, Alexander did not untie the knot but slashed through it with his sword. Another ancient historian says Alexander removed a bolt that separated the knot from the yoke. In either case, Alexander separated the wagon and the yoke. He could claim another sign showing he was meant to be king of Asia.

From Gordium, Alexander turned south and headed back to the coast. One hot day, he took a swim in an icy river fed by the melting snow of nearby mountains. The cold water gave Alexander a chill, followed by a high fever. All but one of the doctors traveling with Alexander's army thought he would die.

One doctor, however, gave the king some medicine, and after several months, Alexander recovered. While Alexander made his way through Phrygia, King Darius III of Persia grew alarmed. He began organizing a huge army in Babylon, an ancient city in what is now Iraq. He wanted to march westward and defeat his Macedonian enemy once and for all. By October 333, Darius had reached Asia Minor and was closing in on the Macedonians. He surprised them by going behind their supply lines instead of meeting them head on. Alexander realized he had to turn back and fight his enemy. The two kings prepared to face each other in battle for the first time. ᴓ

Some historians believe Alexander slashed through the Gordian knot, giving evidence of his upcoming rule of Asia.

5

From a King to a God

⸙∿⸙

Although Alexander was surprised that Darius had sneaked up behind him, he was not unhappy about it. Darius' position, near the town of Issus, gave Alexander the advantage he wanted. Although Darius had a much larger force—perhaps 100,000 men— Alexander would be able to fight the enemy between the Mediterranean Sea and the nearby mountains. In those tight quarters, Darius would find it hard to maneuver his massive army.

In November 333 B.C., Alexander began moving his men north, toward the Persians. As the battle neared, he called together his officers. He reminded them of the great victories they had already won and of the skills they and the Greek fighters possessed. "Our enemies," he said, "are ... men who for centuries

Darius commanded his army from his chariot, which was located in the middle of the front line.

have lived soft and luxurious lives; we of Macedon for generations have been trained in the hard school of danger and war." Although most of the Persian forces were fighting to protect their homeland, Alexander had confidence in his troops. "Our hearts," Alexander said, "will be in it."

The next morning, just before daylight, Alexander prepared his men for battle. They approached the Payas River. On the other side, the Persians waited for their enemy. In his chariot, Darius stood with his best cavalry in the middle of the front Persian line, surrounded by skilled infantry. More cavalry waited on Darius' right, with another line of troops behind him. On the other side, Alexander led cavalry troops on the right end of the Macedonian line. More cavalry were on the left, and in between the horsemen were the feared Macedonian infantry, their sarissas in hand. Alexander and Darius also had small units of archers and javelin throwers ready to launch their artillery when they received the command.

Alexander opened the attack, galloping through the river and into the left side of the Persians' front line. The defense there quickly crumbled, but in the center, the Persians' Greek mercenaries were inflicting heavy damage. Alexander swung his forces into that part of the battle, where he received a slight leg wound. According to the ancient historian Arrian, Darius had already fled the battle by this time. Most

modern historians, however, believe that the Great King fought bravely until he realized that Alexander's forces were too strong. Then Darius fled the battle, and thousands of his men followed him. With Darius' departure, the battle was over—Alexander had won.

The Macedonians defeated Darius and the Persians on the bank of the Issus River.

With the victory, Alexander acquired money and supplies that Darius left behind. The Persian king also fled without his family: his wife, children, and mother, who had accompanied the king on his campaign. After the Battle of Issus, Darius wrote to Alexander, asking him to return the royal family. He now considered Alexander his equal and wanted a friendly relationship. An angry Alexander quickly wrote back. He reminded Darius of the Persian invasions of Greece in the past, which Alexander was now avenging. He accused Darius of the assassination of his father. He also told Darius that the two men were not equal in any way. Alexander now considered himself king of all Asia. Darius could come in person and ask for his family back, as long as he showed the proper respect. Alexander wrote:

Alexander visited the members of Darius' family after his victory at Issus.

If, on the other hand, you wish to dispute your throne, stand and fight for it and do not run away. Wherever you may hide yourself, be sure I will seek you out.

Although he now called himself the king of Asia, Alexander knew his position wasn't solid. Persia still had many troops in other parts of the empire, and his forces had not even come close to the heart of Persia itself. Before going after Darius, Alexander decided to seize control of more of the Persian Empire in the west.

His first major target was the island city of Tyre, off what is now Lebanon. The Tyrians said they were neutral in the war between Alexander and Darius. But they upset Alexander when they refused to let him into the city to make a sacrifice to Heracles. Alexander built a causeway between the mainland and Tyre and then began a siege that lasted for seven months. When he finally entered the city, he killed 6,000 Tyrian soldiers. According to the historian Curtius, 2,000 more "who had survived the rage of the tiring Macedonians, now hung nailed to crosses all along ... the beach."

After Tyre, Alexander won another siege at the city of Gaza in modern Israel. From there, the Macedonian army marched into the heart of Egypt,

> *Despite Darius' request, Alexander refused to release the Persian royalty he had captured. But Alexander treated them well, letting them keep their royal titles and perform traditional Persian religious ceremonies. According to Curtius, the king treated Darius' daughters "with as much respect as if they were his own sisters." After two years in captivity, Stateira, Darius' wife, died. Alexander gave her a lavish funeral.*

a major Persian satrapy. Most Egyptians hated the Persians, so they did not resist Alexander's army. Alexander stopped in Memphis, a city almost 3,000 years old at the time. As great as the Greek culture was, Egypt had created a grand empire thousands of years earlier. One Greek soldier wrote on a wall, "I have gazed on these awesome monuments and am thunderstruck."

In Memphis, Alexander held various contests, bringing in athletes and artists. He also made a sacrifice to a local god. Wherever he went, Alexander respected the religions of the local people to win their support. His attitude also reflected the general Greek tolerance of foreign gods. The Greeks never assumed they had all the answers when it came to something as mysterious as religion.

Shortly after leaving Memphis, Alexander decided to visit a famous oracle located at Siwah in Egypt near what is now Libya. The oracle was dedicated to the Egyptian god Ammon. The Greeks associated this god with their own supreme god, Zeus. Alexander always believed he had a special connection to Zeus, since Zeus was said to be the father of his ancestor Heracles. Now Alexander wanted to learn what the oracle had to say about his future and to follow the footsteps of Heracles, who had also visited Siwah.

Getting to Siwah was risky. It was located in the middle of a desert several hundred miles west

The ancient site of the oracle dedicated to Ammon is in Siwah, Egypt.

of Memphis. After first sailing down the Nile River, Alexander and a small number of his men began to march across the desert. At one point, strong winds

Although he helped plan Alexandria, Alexander never saw any of its buildings, since construction began after he left. After Alexander's death, the city served as the capital of a later Greek empire based in Egypt. Known for its great library, it became a major center of learning. It was the home of a giant lighthouse—one of the seven wonders of the ancient world. For a time, Alexandria declined in size and importance, but today it is a modern city with a population of almost 4 million. In the harbor, scientists have recently found artifacts that date back to the third century B.C.

blew across the hot sands, creating a blinding dust storm. Alexander and his men lost sight of the two guides who were leading them. Suddenly, two crows appeared, and Alexander ordered his men to follow the birds. He believed they had been sent by the gods to lead them to safety. With the crows' help, the men safely reached Siwah.

At the shrine there, Alexander entered a small room and met with the chief priest. Exactly what he asked the oracle is unknown, but the historian Arrian reported that Alexander "received ... the answer which his heart desired." Most likely, the oracle said that Alexander was the son of Zeus. The oracle may have also suggested that Alexander would rule the world. Callisthenes, a writer Alexander brought on the campaign, began to call him Son of Zeus. Alexander may or may not have believed this at the time, but later he accepted the Greeks considering him a god. And it served his purposes as a king to have people believe he was the son of a god, or a god himself. Who would challenge

Lush gardens and magnificent temples were plentiful when ancient Alexandria was at its peak.

someone with such a background?

Leaving Siwah, Alexander reunited with his main army and headed toward the Mediterranean coast. In 331, he founded his first major new city, Alexandria. He later gave other new cities the same name. He modeled Alexandria after the cities of Greece, with a large, open marketplace and temples to many gods. Alexandria became one of the greatest cities of the ancient world.

Despite his active role in designing this new city, Alexander was not an engineer or architect. He was a warrior, and he had unfinished business on the battlefield. Somewhere in Persia, Darius was still alive. And he still claimed to rule land that Alexander now considered his. With Alexander leading the way, the Macedonian army left Egypt, heading for a final showdown with the Persians. ॐ

6 Chapter

RULER
OF PERSIA

❦

While on the march to find Darius, Alexander received a second message from the Great King. Darius offered him money for the safe return of the Persian royal family. He said Alexander could rule lands west of the Euphrates River in what is now Iraq. Darius was also willing to make Alexander a member of his family—he offered to let the Macedonian marry one of his daughters. Parmenion, Alexander's trusted general, learned about Darius' offer. He said, "I would accept those terms if I were Alexander." To the general, the terms seemed fair, and accepting them would avoid a major battle. Alexander replied that he would also accept those terms—if he were Parmenion. But he was the son of a god and a descendant of great Greek heroes, and he would not stop before taking all of Persia.

Darius was forced to retreat to keep his empire intact. He had to rebuild his army in order to challenge Alexander again.

Through the summer of 331 B.C., the Macedonian army closed in on the Persians. The forces that waited for Alexander reflected the size and diversity of Darius' empire. The Great King had Greek infantry and cavalry from Pakistan, Armenia, and other regions. After the defeats at Granicus and Issus, Darius knew he needed a much larger army than Alexander. His cavalry and infantry now outnumbered the Macedonians' by almost five to one. Darius also wanted to fight Alexander where the Persians would have the advantage. Darius would not put himself in a narrow place, as he had at Issus. Instead, the Great King led his men to a plain near Gaugamela. He even prepared the battlefield to his advantage. To make it easier to use his chariots, Darius had his men smooth the fields as much as possible.

After several days of scouting and resting his men, Alexander finally marched his troops into battle. Alexander, wearing armor and a polished iron helmet, rode his prized horse Bucephalas. At the center of the Persian troops were cavalry units. Next to them were elephants, often used in ancient battles to scare enemy horses or trample infantry too slow to get out of their way. The Persians also had many battle chariots. On the wheels were sharp blades called scythes, which could plow through enemy horses and soldiers. Darius commanded the troops from his own chariot.

Exact details of the battle are sketchy because

no eyewitness accounts of that day still exist. The swirling dust of the desert would have made it hard for anyone to see much of the battlefield. But historians know that Alexander had prepared new strategies for this battle against a larger army. At times, the infantry at Gaugamela stood in a box formation, making it harder for the enemy to attack from behind. Alexander also kept some cavalry hidden among the infantry positioned on the far sides. These horsemen would be used for counterattacks.

The battle began with the Persian cavalry charging into the right of Alexander's line. Soon horsemen on both sides were fighting on the left, as well. Shouts and the clattering of metal weapons filled the air, while arrows and javelins sailed over

The scythes sticking out of the Persian chariots were feared by the Greek and Macedonian infantry.

the soldiers' heads and into their targets. Alexander led one counterattack toward the Persian center. The Macedonians and Greeks formed a wedge that drove through a gap in the enemy's lines. Both infantry and cavalry began to slaughter the panicking Persians. Alexander and some of his men pressed on, looking for Darius. Arrian, writing almost 300 years later, said that Darius "saw nothing but terrors all around him, [and] was the first to turn tail and ride for safety." With their Great King gone, the Persians lost their will to fight. Many ran off, while others were killed by the advancing Macedonians and Greeks.

Once again, Alexander and his men had defeated a much larger army and forced Darius to flee. Although Alexander would have to track down the Great King, he knew that no army in central Asia could defeat him, and Persia was his.

After the battle at Gaugamela, Alexander stopped in Babylon for a month. He then marched to Susa, the winter home of Persia's kings. Alexander needed to control the main cities of Persia to assert his authority and take the vast amount of money and valuables Darius had amassed. When Alexander reached Susa, the local satrap did not challenge him. Instead, he greeted Alexander warmly and gave him gifts, including camels and elephants. In the city, Alexander found statues the Persians had stolen when they raided Greece 150 years earlier. He sent

the statues back to Athens. Alexander also sat in the throne that Darius and other Persian rulers had used. Because Alexander was so short compared to the Persian kings, his feet dangled in the air. An aide quickly placed a stool under his feet so the king would not look like a child sitting in a grown-up's chair.

From Susa, the Macedonian forces continued east. Alexander's next goal was the heart of Persia and its capital, Persepolis. But first, he and his men had to cut through mountainous lands guarded by a local tribe, the Uxians. They demanded a toll, just as they always did from anyone crossing through their land, including Darius. Alexander said he would pay the toll, but instead he sent some of his men on a sneak attack. Other troops took position on a ridge where the Uxians would most likely retreat. In less than a day, Alexander defeated the Uxians, who then agreed to pay him an annual tribute.

Proceeding through the mountains, Alexander came to a pass called the Persian Gates. The local satrap had amassed a huge defensive force to stop the Macedonians' advance. Fighting from higher ground, the Persians showered their enemy with catapult shots. For once, Alexander was forced to retreat. But using information he gathered from Persian prisoners, he learned of another pass. Alexander took some of his men through the narrow, rocky passage. At the same time, other Greeks and Macedonians stayed where they were to keep the Persians' attention. Using a trumpet as a signal, the two forces then attacked the Persians at the same time. Once again, Alexander showed his ability to make quick decisions on the battlefield.

Passing through the Persian Gates, Alexander dashed toward Persepolis, reaching the capital in January 330. He let his men go wild, allowing them to rob homes and massacre civilians. Alexander

According to Diodorus, Alexander showed one of his great acts of kindness on the road to Persepolis. He met a group of old Greek soldiers who had been taken as prisoners by the Persians. The Persians had disfigured them, chopping off limbs, ears, and noses. Alexander cried while talking to the men, and he gave each of them money, clothing, oxen, sheep, and 50 bushels of wheat. He also said the men would never have to pay taxes again.

saw the violence as payback for the Persians' earlier attacks on Greece. The ancient historian Diodorus described the scene of violence: "Such was their over-powering lust for loot that they ended up fighting each other for it."

The Macedonians and Greeks stayed in Persepolis for several months. Finally, in April, Alexander learned that Darius was farther east, in a region called Media. The Great King had gone to Ecbatana, another home to Persia's kings. Darius hoped he could raise another army and fight Alexander again. But by now, thanks to his conquests, Alexander was the richest man in the world. He could field a much larger army than Darius, and he had begun to win the loyalty of the Persians he had already defeated. Alexander wisely left Persians in charge of the satrapies he

Persepolis was the heart of the Persian Empire.

conquered, giving them a share of the power. They began to realize that their best course was to support Alexander. Just to make sure, Alexander always left a Macedonian officer behind to watch the satraps.

Before leaving Persepolis, Alexander burned the city's royal palaces. The action may have been deliberate, or it may have been the result of one of Alexander's drunken parties. Some suggested that during a party at one of the palaces, Alexander accepted a young woman's suggestion to let her and her friends burn the building. Whatever happened, Alexander later seemed to regret his decision. After all, the palaces now belonged to him, not Darius.

Heading toward Ecbatana, Alexander met a member of the Persian ruling class. He informed the king that many leading Persians supported his rule and that Darius had only been able to recruit a small army. Since he did not need a huge force, Alexander sent some of the troops home and some to Ecbatana. He then led his smaller army along Darius' trail. Eager to track down the Persian, Alexander drove his men hard. Arrian reported that "many of the men, unable to stand the pace, dropped out, and a number of horses were worked to death."

Meanwhile, some of Darius' men deserted him and sided with Alexander. The king now realized that Darius' shrinking force could move faster than his own army, so Alexander would not be able to overtake

Darius' killers were members of his own elite, men supposedly loyal to the Persian king.

them. He decided to let his men rest for several days. But when he heard several local satraps had arrested Darius, he resumed the hunt again. At times, the men marched through the night, and Alexander was soon just one day behind Darius and his captors. In July, the Macedonians found Darius nearing death. The men who had arrested him had wounded him and then fled before Alexander could catch them.

Some later believed Alexander did not want Darius to die. He was willing to let Darius play some role in his government, although Alexander would be the king. When Darius died, Alexander honored him by sending his body back to Persepolis. The former Great King was buried in the royal tomb. Meanwhile, the new king of Asia prepared for more conquests. ℘

A. Castaigne

7 TROUBLES OF A CONQUEROR

❦

With Darius dead, most of Alexander's men assumed the war was over. They hoped to return to Greece and their families. Alexander, however, convinced them their work wasn't done. Persian allies in the east didn't accept Alexander as their king, and Bessus, one of the men who had killed Darius, was on the loose. He and an army had fled into Bactria, part of what is now Afghanistan. Bessus declared that he was the rightful king of Asia. With his army now back to full strength, Alexander began to pursue Bessus.

But even before confronting Bessus, Alexander dealt with a troubling event within his own camp. In October 330 B.C., Alexander learned that some of his men were plotting to kill him. Alexander had upset some of his commanders with his behavior in Asia.

He seemed to be losing touch with his Macedonian culture and acting more like a Persian. He began wearing Persian clothes, and he took on Persians as guards. Some of the plotters may have also been upset with Alexander's decision to keep going farther into Asia. But before the plotters could strike, Alexander learned of their plan and had them arrested.

One of the men arrested was Philotas, commander of the cavalry and the son of Parmenion. Philotas may not have actually wanted to kill Alexander, but he knew about the plot and didn't tell the king about it. Alexander executed Philotas and then executed Parmenion, as well. The old general probably didn't know about the plot, but Alexander didn't want to risk Parmenion turning against him to avenge his son's death.

After Philotas' execution, the Macedonians headed south and camped for 60 days. Then Alexander resumed his pursuit of Bessus. His men marched across Afghanistan

Around the time of the trial of Philotas, local villagers called Mardians stole Bucephalas, Alexander's horse. Some historians say that the king loved his mount more than all the people in his life, except perhaps for his mother and his best friend, Hephaestion. According to Plutarch, "Alexander was enraged and ... [threatened] that unless [the Mardians] gave back his horse, he would exterminate the whole tribe, together with their women and children." Quickly, some of the Mardians brought Bucephalas to Alexander, along with other gifts to appease the angry king.

After Philotas was arrested and killed at the order of Alexander, the troops began to wonder if his death was necessary.

and over the Hindu Kush, a rugged mountain range. The army struggled to move through the heavy spring snow, and the historian Arrian noted that "his men suffered severely from exhaustion and lack of supplies." Bessus tried to slow down Alexander by destroying villages where the Macedonians might find food. Still, the army pressed on, surprising Bessus with its speed under such difficult conditions.

Alexander never fought a decisive battle with Bessus. Some of the Persian officers sent word to Alexander that they would arrest Bessus and turn him over rather than fight. Once Alexander had Bessus in his hands, he had him tortured and killed. But even with Bessus dead, Alexander still faced difficulties in this remote part of the Persian Empire. Local tribesmen began to rebel, and fighting in the mountainous terrain was sometimes difficult.

Because he murdered Darius, Bessus was executed according to Persian tradition.

Alexander used his siege engines to take control of some forts in the region. At other times, he tricked his

enemy. With the Scythians, fierce horsemen of Central Asia, he sent in infantry as decoys. The Scythians then used their usual tactic, shooting arrows at their enemy while riding around them in a circle. With the Scythians distracted, Alexander's cavalry then rode onto the scene and inflicted heavy casualties. In the end, the Scythian king agreed to accept Alexander's rule.

In 328, while fighting in the region of Sogdia in what is now part of modern Uzbekistan, Alexander was said to have fallen in love. A woman named Roxane was among the captives taken after one conquest. The Macedonians said she was the most beautiful woman in Asia, next to Darius' wife. Alexander decided to marry her, though the decision could have been partly political. By marrying the daughter of a local commander, Alexander could win the support of the people.

Also in 328, Alexander lost Cleitus, another one of his most experienced generals. But this time, the king had only himself to blame. Alexander and his men

Some historians have wondered why Alexander waited so long to choose a bride. With his power, he could have married any woman, and he met many worthy royal women before meeting Roxane. Perhaps Roxane was the only woman who, as Arrian wrote, led the king to feel "love at first sight." Alexander did have a longtime girlfriend, Barsine, and together they had a son, Heracles. After marrying Roxane, he had several more brides. Some modern historians think that Alexander also enjoyed the company of men, which was common among Greek men of the time.

were attending a banquet in Maracanda—now called Samarkand. Once again, wine flowed freely, and the officers were soon drunk. Cleitus, like some of the other Macedonians, was not happy with Alexander's taste for Asian culture. He also disliked the way some of the men flattered the young king.

At one point in the evening, Cleitus spoke out, saying the Macedonians as an army, not Alexander alone, had won many great victories. The king's supporters then said Philip, Alexander's father, had never done anything as great as Alexander had. Now Cleitus exploded with anger. He had served under Philip and knew the old king's great skills. He also reminded Alexander that he, Cleitus, had saved Alexander's life several times during battle.

Alexander, fueled by rage and alcohol, lashed out at Cleitus. The historian Plutarch wrote that the king cried out:

> *You scum! Do you think you can keep on speaking of me like this ... and not pay for it?*

The two men continued to argue, while others in the hall tried to calm them down. Finally, Alexander grabbed a spear from one of his guards and killed Cleitus. Instantly filled with regret, Alexander then tried to kill himself, realizing what he had done to one

of his most trusted advisers. His men had to restrain him, and for the next three days, Alexander wept for Cleitus, refusing to eat or drink.

Alexander's temper and drunkenness drove him to murder Cleitus, one of his best generals.

The death of Cleitus illustrated several troubling issues. Alexander's embrace of Persian ways helped him gain friends in Asia, but it upset some of the Macedonians. And his anger and drinking seemed to be getting worse as time went on. Still, Alexander did not change his ways, and his behavior continued to trouble some of his men.

After putting down new rebellions in and around Sogdia through 328, Alexander stirred new grumbling among the Macedonians and Greeks. He wanted his subjects to follow the Persian tradition of *proskynesis*, a term referring to the act of prostration, or laying down at the king's feet. For the Greeks, however, proskynesis was part of religious ceremonies as a way to show respect to the gods. Humans never practiced proskynesis with each other, they argued. To Alexander's critics, the demand for prostration was another sign that he was becoming too Persian. It also seemed to show that Alexander did consider himself the son of a god rather than the son of a human father.

Callisthenes, Alexander's historian, dared to challenge the king on proskynesis, saying:

> *When you are home again, do you really propose to force the Greeks, who love their liberty more than anyone else in the world, to prostrate themselves before you? Or will you let the Greeks off and impose this shameful duty on the Macedonians?*

Alexander disliked this comment, but he decided it was not worth angering his men. They would not have to prostrate themselves before him, but the Persians would.

Shortly after this, another plot to murder Alexander emerged. Callisthenes was accused of being part of it, though modern historians doubt this. In any event, he and several royal pages serving with Alexander were killed. With order restored, Alexander prepared for his next goal: India. ✒

Callisthenes recorded the details of Alexander's conquests. He was also taught by Aristotle.

Chapter

8

THE FAR EDGE OF THE EMPIRE

ແ໑ຂຈ

Aristotle, Alexander's great teacher, had believed that looking east from the Hindu Kush, a person could see an ocean that marked the end of Earth. But as Alexander looked down from those peaks, he saw nothing but land. Now he hoped to reach the ocean that marked the farthest boundary of Asia. To do that, he would have to conquer India, territory that was mostly a mystery to the Greeks.

Darius had held loose control over lands up to the Indus River that provided the Persians with gold and other valuable resources. In the spring of 327 B.C., Alexander began his march into those lands. His army now included mercenary cavalry from Central Asia, as well as fresh troops from Greece and Macedonia who had marched for almost a year to reach their

Alexander was probably the first Greek to gaze from the peaks of the Hindu Kush.

king. Alexander divided his force, giving Hephaestion command of the main army. These troops marched through the Khyber Pass, a famous mountain pass between Afghanistan and Pakistan. Alexander led the rest of the army on a more northerly route.

Alexander fought several small battles as he traveled through a region called Massaga. At one point, an arrow hit him, but the wound was minor. In the spring of 326, Alexander linked up with Hephaestion at the west side of the Indus River. Hephaestion's men had already built a bridge of boats across the river. The Taxiles, local people who lived on the other side of the Indus, had brought gifts for the king, including elephants. Across the Indus, the Taxiles provided 5,000 troops for his army.

Alexander then headed for the Hydaspes River. Waiting on the other side was Porus, ruler of a rich kingdom. Alexander had sent word that Porus should meet him and pay a tribute. Instead, Porus arrived with an army to stop the foreigners' advance.

Alexander had about 80,000 troops, while Porus had less than half that. Still, Porus had placed his men in a good defensive position, and his forces included up to 200 war elephants. As in past battles, Alexander had to move his men across a river to fight. This time, however, he faced a wide, deep river. The time of year also worked against Alexander. Snow in the nearby mountains was melting, boosting the river's depth and speed. Crossing before the waters receded could be dangerous. The enemy's elephants would scare the Macedonians' horses, adding to their difficulties. Since Alexander did not want to wait until the river would be lower, he created a plan that fooled his enemy and gave him the advantage. Alexander split his army in two, keeping the smaller force across from Porus' army to hold their attention. The soldiers constantly moved along the riverbank, acting as if

Porus gathered his war elephants in preparation for the war with Alexander.

Ancient coins still exist showing scenes from the Battle of Hydaspes. One shows Alexander riding Bucephalas as he attacks Porus, who sits on a war elephant. Other surviving coins from Alexander's era show him as a god. These coins help historians understand how Alexander was seen by others—or how he wanted them to see him. In general, ancient coins give evidence of a society's art, politics, and culture.

they were preparing an assault. At first, Porus carefully watched these movements. When an attack never came, he began to ignore them. This gave Alexander the chance to lead his other force 15 miles (24 km) up the river without being seen.

Just before dawn on a late spring morning, Alexander began to take his men across the Hydaspes. Porus' scouts had seen Alexander's advance, and the son of the Indian king arrived with a force of about 2,000 men and 120 chariots. Alexander successfully defeated this advance unit, killing Porus' son in the process. Porus then sent his main army against Alexander, leaving a smaller force to try to keep the rest of the Macedonians from crossing the river.

The Battle of Hydaspes was one of the fiercest Alexander ever fought. His enemy skillfully used the war elephants to keep the Macedonian cavalry from launching an effective attack. Later, the elephants inflicted heavy damage on the infantry. But with a larger force, Alexander was able to kill or wound many of the fearsome beasts. His troops also defeated the enemy cavalry. When the battle ended, Porus had lost as many as 15,000 men, while only about 1,000 Macedonians had been killed.

For Alexander, the greatest loss was the death of Bucephalas. Some said say the horse died of wounds he suffered during the battle. Arrian, however, claimed the animal died of old age. In either case, the king buried his horse and then founded a new city in his honor. He named it Bucephala.

After the battle, Alexander and Porus met. Alexander studied his opponent and then spoke: "What do you wish that I should do with you?" Porus replied, "Treat me as a king ought."

Alexander accepted the surrender of Porus after the Battle of Hydaspes.

Alexander liked this response. He saw that Porus was a noble man, worthy of respect even in defeat. Alexander decided to let him keep his lands, thus winning Porus' loyalty. Other local chieftains and rulers also accepted Alexander's rule. Porus' cousin, however, refused to acknowledge Alexander's conquest and fled eastward with a small army. Alexander pursued him to the Hyphasis River, almost 400 miles (640 km) west of the Hydaspes.

The march east was difficult—perhaps the worst the Macedonians had faced. India's monsoon season had arrived, and rain fell endlessly for weeks. During this time, the men battled Indians who resisted Alexander's rule. The fighting was sometimes cruel; Alexander even ordered the killing of hundreds of sick civilians. When the men heard reports about the Indian armies waiting to fight them on the other side of the Hyphasis River, the soldiers began complaining.

Alexander knew the men were upset and tried to lift their spirits. He gave a long speech that reminded them of their past glories and the successes that still waited for them in India. "When all Asia is overrun ... the utmost hopes of riches or power which each one of you cherishes will be far surpassed," he said. But Alexander added that if anyone wanted to go home, they could. The speech didn't inspire the men as Alexander had hoped. They were tired of war and being away from home. Coenus, an officer, found the courage to address

Alexander was unable to convince his restless and frustrated troops to continue fighting.

the king: "Sir, if there is one thing above all others a successful man should know, it is when to stop."

The other men present applauded Coenus, but Alexander became angry. For several days, he sat in his tent, hoping the men would change their minds, but they did not budge. Finally, Alexander was convinced it was time to go home. The soldiers wept with joy when they heard the news and asked the gods to bless their king. But for Alexander, in the words of Arrian, it was "the only defeat he had ever suffered." Before leaving, Alexander had his men build 12 altars to honor the 12 major Greek gods. The spot marked the farthest reach of Alexander's empire in Asia. ℘

9 THE END OF A KING

❦

Alexander and his men returned to the Hydaspes River to prepare for their long journey home. The fighting, however, was not over. Alexander had just received reinforcements, so his army was now about 120,000 soldiers strong. He planned to sail down the Hydaspes to the Indus, conquering as he went. His men had amassed a fleet of almost 1,000 ships for this new mission. Some of the troops would sail under the command of Nearchus, one of Alexander's generals. The others would march along the river's shores.

The Macedonians departed in November 326 B.C. Their first enemy was the Mallians. Alexander caught them by surprise and killed thousands before they could mount a defense. Then the Macedonians put the enemy's cities under siege. At one fortress, Alexander

The Greek warships were light and easily maneuverable, making them invaluable in battle.

scrambled up a ladder to the top of the wall, then leapt down into the city below. According to Arrian, the king hoped his brave act would startle the enemy, and if he died, his courage would be remembered forever. Three other soldiers eventually joined Alexander inside the fortress. During the fighting, an arrow pierced Alexander's armor and entered his lung. He lost a lot of blood, and his men carried him off on his shield.

When the battle ended, rumors swept through the Macedonian camp that Alexander was dead. He remained out of sight for several days, healing from the wound. Finally, to ease the men's fears, the king appeared before them and climbed onto a horse. The soldiers were relieved to see he was all right.

With the defeat of the Mallians, neighboring tribes came to pay their respects to Alexander. The local kings greeted Alexander with gifts rather than fight his fearsome troops. The Indians did not want to experience the

Alexander first met Nearchus when they were boys in Macedonia. As the admiral of Alexander's India fleet, Nearchus kept a journal, and parts of it were later used as a source by the historian Arrian. The voyage west was dangerous as the fleet sailed through unknown waters. In addition, Nearchus didn't receive the supplies Alexander had promised. On land, when Alexander saw Nearchus for the first time, he didn't recognize the admiral. Nearchus' hair was long and tangled, he was covered with salt, and he had lost weight. Alexander was thrilled to hear him say, "Sir, your ships and men are safe."

massive slaughter the invaders had inflicted on the
Mallians. The dead included many women and children, and the Mallians who survived were enslaved.

After scattered fighting along the way, Alexander
reached the Indian Ocean in the summer of 325. He
now planned for the journey home. His fleet would
sail across the Indian Ocean and through the Persian
Gulf to Babylonia in modern-day Iraq. One part of his
army would take a northern land route. Alexander,
meanwhile, would march the rest of the men through
Gedrosia, in what is now southern Pakistan. The

*A surgeon
removed an
arrow from
Alexander's
side. Although
he lost a lot
of blood,
Alexander was
able to recover
completely.*

trip would take the men through a brutal desert. According to Arrian, Alexander knew the route was dangerous, but the king wanted to stay fairly close to the shoreline and his fleet. Alexander, as always, was driven by ambition. Other kings had tried to cross this desert and failed. Alexander wanted to be the first to succeed.

The march through the desert was hard on his men. They could not always find water, and to avoid the broiling sun, they marched at night. Most of the horses and mules died along the way, and the men quickly butchered them for food. If soldiers fell sick, they were left on the sand to recover—or die. Even some of the water they found proved deadly. Sudden monsoon rains could cause small streams to flood, and the rushing waters carried away many of the wives and children who traveled with the soldiers.

Finally, the troops reached Pura, the capital of Gedrosia, and the rest of Alexander's army soon rejoined him. During this time, Alexander heard reports of satraps abusing their power in their territories. Some robbed local temples or used violence against their citizens. Alexander had some of these satraps executed for their crimes. Then the king once again split up his army, with Hephaestion leading most of the men through southern Persia. Alexander took a slightly more northerly route to Persepolis, the old Persian capital. From there, the reunited army headed to Susa.

In that city, Alexander arranged a grand mass wedding. He, Hephaestion, and 90 other leading officers married members of the Persian royalty. Alexander took two brides, including Stateira, the daughter of Darius III, the late Great King. Alexander wanted to clearly link the ruling class of Macedonia and Greece with the Persian royalty. To mark the celebration, Alexander also paid off any debts his men had incurred during their service in Asia.

Once again, some of the Macedonians disliked Alexander's good relations with the Persians and his acceptance of their culture. Later, in the summer of 324, he angered more men when he announced he

Alexander's marriage to Stateira further tested the troops' tolerance for Persian culture.

was forcing older soldiers to retire. The army was now in the town of Opis, north of Babylon, and the men revolted again. Alexander reacted angrily, but this time he executed the officers who led the revolt. Then he delivered another long speech, attacking the men for their disloyalty. He pointed out all that his father Philip and he had done for them and for Greece. He reminded them that he had suffered just as they had in battle. "There is no part of my body," he said, "but my back which has not a scar." When he finished, Alexander stormed off, leaving the men stunned.

Alexander had an option now that he did not have when the men first revolted in India. He could replace his Greek and Macedonian troops with Persians. When his men learned he planned to do that, their mutiny quickly crumbled. They begged Alexander for his forgiveness. With tears in his eyes, he granted it.

In the fall of 324, Alexander went to Ecbatana. There he held a festival with games and artistic contests. During the festival, Hephaestion became ill. Rather than follow his doctor's orders, the general continued to celebrate, eating and drinking heavily. Within a few days, he was dead. Alexander wailed at the loss of his best friend and refused to eat for several days. When he finally recovered, Alexander did what he liked best. He waged war. He led his forces against the Cossaeans, a tribe in the nearby

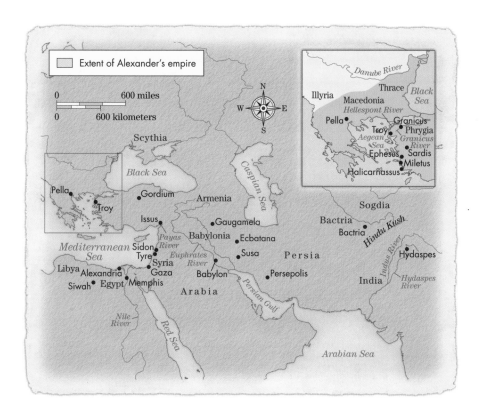

Extent of Alexander's empire

0   600 miles

0   600 kilometers

Scythia

Black Sea

Pella

Troy

Gordium

Armenia

Caspian Sea

Issus

Gaugamela

Payas River

Babylonia

Ecbatana

Mediterranean Sea

Sidon

Euphrates River

Susa

Persia

Tyre

Syria

Libya

Alexandria

Gaza

Babylon

Persepolis

India

Hydaspes River

Siwah

Egypt

Memphis

Arabia

Persian Gulf

Nile River

Red Sea

Arabian Sea

Sogdia

Bactria

Bactria

Hindu Kush

Indus River

Hydaspes

Danube River

Illyria

Thrace

Black Sea

Macedonia

Hellespont River

Pella

Troy

Granicus

Phrygia

Aegean Sea

Granicus River

Ephesus

Sardis

Miletus

Halicarnassus

Alexander's Macedonian Empire included most of the Persian Empire.

mountains. By one account, he killed all the males in the tribe as a sacrifice to Hephaestion. In that instance, Alexander's cruelty and capacity for love were combined.

As 323 began, he made his way to Babylon. Nearchus met him there, and the two men planned for Alexander's next military campaign. Although the Macedonians had stopped their eastern Asian conquest, Alexander now had his eye on Arabia. By some reports, he also wanted to invade North Africa and Sicily. Alexander ordered the harbor of Babylon to be expanded because he wanted to build another 1,000-ship fleet for this new campaign.

As the planning went on, Alexander attended another of the drinking parties he so enjoyed. According to the historian Diodorus, the king drank one huge cup of wine in a single gulp. "Instantly he cried aloud as if pierced by a violent pain." Other sources say that he fell ill after the celebration and his health failed slowly. In either case, Alexander died on June 10, 323. His body was buried in Egypt. It was originally buried in Memphis before it was moved to Alexandria.

The cause of Alexander's death is one of the great unsolved mysteries of ancient history. Some scholars believe he died from alcohol poisoning. Others think he caught a disease that ancient medicine could not cure. Or perhaps his wound fighting the Mallians never healed properly and it somehow ruined his health. Some of Alexander's friends suggested he was poisoned. Whatever killed Alexander, he died without a clear successor. His generals had gathered around his deathbed and asked to whom he was leaving his immense, hard-won kingdom. His simple answer: "To the strongest."

The Macedonian Empire was eventually split into several parts. Ptolemy, one of Alexander's bodyguards, founded a kingdom based in Egypt that lasted for almost three centuries. The general

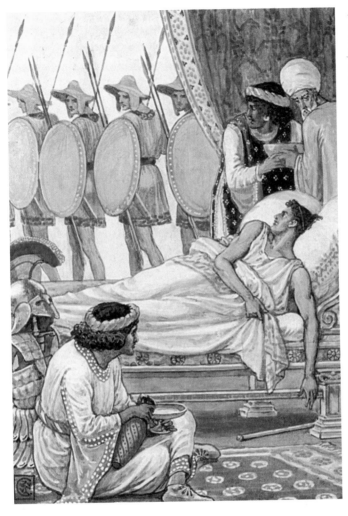

Seleucus created a kingdom centered in the heart of Persia. It stretched from what is now eastern Turkey to Afghanistan. Another kingdom was based in the Macedonian homeland. It was ruled by Antigonus, another general. A small kingdom in western Turkey, Pergamum, was ruled by a prince called Attalus.

After Alexander's death, his relatives and generals battled each other for the kingdom. His wife Roxane had a son, Alexander IV, who was named after his father and was the rightful king from his birth. Roxane hoped her son would live to rule on his own accord. Instead, both Alexander IV and his mother were murdered. Heracles, the king's son with Barsine, followed the same fate.

These kingdoms continued Greek influence in the lands Alexander had conquered. Eventually, the Macedonian Empire was ruled by Antigonus Gonatas, the grandson of Alexander's general, Antigonus.

Alexander had always respected strength in himself and others. He had shown it many times on the battlefield. At times, he had also shown cruelty. His sieges and battles killed tens of thousands of innocent civilians. But Alexander lived in a time when rulers assumed that their power let them do whatever they wanted. And he was not merely a king. In his mind, he was the son of a god—and the greatest warrior the world had ever known.

Both ancient and modern historians have seen another side to Alexander the Great. Some have described him as a man who was kind to women, felt strong emotions, and could forgive people who wronged him. Arrian wrote, "[O]f all the monarchs of old, [Alexander] was the only one who had the nobility of heart to be sorry for his mistakes."

With his conquests, Alexander helped deepen the contacts between the Greek world and Asia.

The emperial Ottoman Museum in Constantinople holds an ancient sarcophagus with images of Alexander displayed on the sides.

Greek writings and ideas have spread far beyond the Aegean Sea. Because of Alexander's conquests, Greek became the language of the early Christian church, as it developed in the lands he had conquered. His military example influenced future European conquerors, such as the Romans. Julius Caesar, the great Roman general, supposedly wept when he thought about all Alexander had done at such a young age. Caesar knew he would never be able to match him.

Interest in Alexander remains strong. During the 1990s, an English television crew followed his footsteps from Macedonia to India. In 2004, a major U.S. film depicted highlights of his life. Alexander's achievements and his drive for glory will always keep his memory alive. ✑

ALEXANDER'S LIFE

343 B.C.

Studies with Aristotle at Mieza

356 B.C.

Born on July 20, in Pella, Macedonia

350 B.C.

347 B.C.

The great philosopher Plato dies

356 B.C.

The temple of Delphi, the Greeks' holiest shrine, is destroyed in the Sacred War

WORLD EVENTS

339 B.C.

Puts down a
rebellion in
Macedonia—
his first victory
in battle

338 B.C.

Helps his
father, King
Philip II, defeat
the Greeks
at Chaeronea

336 B.C.

Becomes king
of Macedonia
when his father
is assassinated

340 B.C.

338 B.C.

King Artaxerxes IV
ascends to the Persian
throne after his father
is murdered

ALEXANDER'S LIFE

334 B.C.

Defeats Persian
forces at the
Granicus River

333 B.C.

Defeats Darius III,
ruler of Persia, at
the Battle of Issus

332 B.C.

Enters Egypt
and is greeted
as its new ruler

335 B.C.

335 B.C.

Aristotle founds the
Lyceum, a school in
Athens that is the birth-
place of western science
and philosophy

333 B.C.

Greek philosopher
Zeno of Citium,
called the father of
stoicism, is born

WORLD EVENTS

331 B.C.

Visits the oracle
at Siwah; founds
Alexandria, Egypt;
defeats Darius III
at the Battle of
Gaugamela

330 B.C.

Executes men
accused of
plotting to
kill him

330 B.C.

330 B.C.

Darius III, king
of Persia, is
murdered by
his captors

ALEXANDER'S LIFE

326 B.C.

Defeats Porus at the Battle of the Hydaspes; ends Indian campaign

328 B.C.

Kills one of his own generals in an argument

327 B.C.

Marries Roxane, his first wife; begins invasion of India

329 B.C.

The Circus Maximus, a huge arena, is completed in Rome

WORLD EVENTS

323 B.C.

Dies in Babylon and his successors begin to carve up his empire

324 B.C.

Marries Stateira and Parysatis

325 B.C.

Suffers serious wound in battle with the Mallians

325 B.C.

Greek explorer Pytheas of Massilia (present-day Marseille, France) makes the first recorded visit by a Greek to what is now Great Britain

322 B.C.

Aristotle dies

DATE OF BIRTH: July 20, 356 B.C.

BIRTHPLACE: Pella, Macedonia

FATHER: Philip II
(382–336 B.C.)

MOTHER: Olympias
(c. 375–316 B.C.)

EDUCATION: Tutored by Aristotle

CHILD: Heracles (c. 327–309 B.C.)
(with Barsine)

FIRST SPOUSE: Roxane (c. 343–310 B.C.)

DATE OF MARRIAGE: 327 B.C.

CHILD: Alexander IV
(323–310 B.C.)

SECOND SPOUSE: Stateira (363–309 B.C.)

DATE OF MARRIAGE: 324 B.C.

THIRD SPOUSE: Parysatis

DATE OF MARRIAGE: 324 B.C.

DATE OF DEATH: June 10, 323 B.C.

PLACE OF BURIAL: Alexandria, Egypt
(originally buried
numerous places)

Further Reading

Adams, Simon. *Alexander: The Boy Soldier Who Conquered the World*. Washington, D.C.: National Geographic, 2005.

Buxton, Richard. *The Complete World of Greek Mythology*. London: Thames & Hudson, 2004.

Crompton, Samuel Willard. *Alexander the Great*. Broomall, Pa.: Chelsea House, 2004.

Nardo, Don. *A History of the Ancient Greeks*. San Diego: Lucent Books, 2004.

Reece, Katherine E. *The Persians: Warriors of the Ancient World*. Vero Beach, Fla.: Rourke Pub., 2005.

Skelton, Debra, and Pamela Dell. *Empire of Alexander the Great*. New York: Facts on File, 2005.

Stefoff, Rebecca. *The Ancient Mediterranean*. New York: Benchmark Books, 2005.

Look for more Signature Lives books about this era:

Aristotle: *Philosopher, Teacher, and Scientist*
ISBN: 0-7565-1873-3

Socrates: *Ancient Greek in Search of the Truth*
ISBN: 0-7565-1874-1

Thucydides: *Ancient Greek Historian*
ISBN: 0-7565-1875-X

On the Web

For more information on
Alexander the Great, use FactHound.

1. Go to *www.facthound.com*
2. Type in a search word related to this
   book or this book ID: 0756518725
3. Click on the *Fetch It* button.

FactHound will find the best
Web sites for you.

Historic Sites

The University of Pennsylvania Musuem
of Archaeology and Anthropology
3260 South St.
Philadelphia, PA 19104
215/898-4000
Exhibits on ancient Greece

The Metropolitan Museum of Art
1000 Fifth Ave.
New York, NY 10028
212/535-7710
Artifacts, statues, and literature from
ancient Greece

B.C.
a Christian term meaning "before Christ" and referring to dates that occurred before the birth of Jesus; B.C. dates decrease as time goes on

cavalry
soldiers who fight on horseback

city-states
independent cities that also rule over the surrounding countryside

counterattack
military action taken after an enemy has struck first

Hellenic
relating to Greece or the Greeks, from the Greek word _Hellene_, meaning "Greek"

mercenary
a soldier who fights for money for any army

omen
a sign indicating what will happen in the future

razed
completely flattened or destroyed

sarissa
a long spear with sharp points at each end

satrapy
region of land run by an official in the Persian Empire

seer
a person who can predict future events

tribute
money paid by one nation to keep a more powerful nation from attacking

Source Notes

Chapter 1

Page 11, line 1: Arrian. *Anabasis of Alexander, Books I–IV*. Trans. P.A. Brunt. Great Britain: St. Edmundsbury Press Ltd., 1976, p. 253.

Page 12, line 5: Arrian. *The Campaigns of Alexander*. Trans. Aubrey de Sélincourt. New York: Dorset Press, 1971, p. 163.

Chapter 2

Page 16, line 28: Plutarch. *The Age of Alexander: Nine Greek Lives*. Trans. Ian Scott-Kilvert. London: Penguin Books, 1973, p. 255.

Page 21, line 6: Guy MacLean Rogers. *Alexander: The Ambiguity of Greatness*. New York: Random House, 2004, p. 6.

Page 22, line 6: *The Age of Alexander: Nine Greek Lives*, p. 257.

Page 22, line 14: Ibid.

Page 23, line 1: Ibid., p. 258.

Chapter 3

Page 26, line 6: Ibid., p. 256.

Page 28, line 5: "The Battle of Chaeronea." *Livius.org* 11 April 2006. 15 Jan. 2006. www.livius.org/aj-al/alexander/alexander_t42.html

Page 31, line 1: *The Age of Alexander: Nine Greek Lives*, p. 261.

Page 33, line 16: N.G.L. Hammond. *The Genius of Alexander the Great*. Chapel Hill, N.C.: University of North Carolina Press, 1997, p. 27.

Chapter 4

Page 36, line 26: *The Age of Alexander: Nine Greek Lives*, p. 266.

Page 37, line 10: Waldemar Heckel and John Yardley. *Alexander the Great: Historical Sources in Translation*. Malden, Mass.: Blackwell Publishing, 2004, p. 37.

Page 38, line 16: *The Genius of Alexander the Great*, p. 64.

Page 40, line 5: *The Campaigns of Alexander*, p. 71.

Page 41, line 9: Ibid., p. 76.

Chapter 5

Page 47, line 15: Ibid., p. 112.

Page 48, line 5: Ibid.

Page 50, line 8: Ibid., p. 128.

Page 51, sidebar: *Alexander the Great: Historical Sources in Translation*, p. 194.

Page 51, line 23: Ibid., p. 153.

Page 52, line 6: Michael Wood. *In the Footsteps of Alexander the Great: A Journey from Greece to Asia*. Berkeley: University of California Press, 1997, p. 71.

Page 54, line 16: *The Campaigns of Alexander*, p. 71.

Chapter 6

Page 57, line 9: *The Age of Alexander: Nine Greek Lives*, p. 285.

Page 60, line 8: *The Campaigns of Alexander*, p. 169.

Page 63, line 3: *In the Footsteps of Alexander the Great: A Journey from Greece to Asia*, p. 110.

Page 64, line 22: *The Campaigns of Alexander*, p. 182.

Chapter 7

Page 68, sidebar: *The Age of Alexander: Nine Greek Lives*, p. 301.

Page 69, line 3: *The Campaigns of Alexander*, p. 194.

Page 71, sidebar: Ibid., p. 234.

Page 72, line 19: *The Age of Alexander: Nine Greek Lives*, p. 308.

Page 74, line 24: *The Campaigns of Alexander*, p. 221.

Chapter 8

Page 81, line 11: Ibid., p. 281.

Page 82, line 22: Ibid., p. 295.

Page 83, line 1: Ibid., p. 297.

Page 83, line 10: Ibid., p. 298.

Chapter 9

Page 86, sidebar: "Arrian, Anabasis Alexandri: Book VIII (Indica)." Trans. E. Iliff Robson. *University of Kwazulu-Natal.* 15 Jan. 2006. www.und.ac.za/und/classics/india/arrian/htm

Page 90, line 9: *The Campaigns of Alexander*, p. 363.

Page 92, line 6: P.C. Doherty. *The Death of Alexander the Great: Who—or What—Killed the Young Conqueror of the Known World?* New York: Carroll & Graf Publishers, 2004, p. 60.

Page 92, line 23: *Alexander the Great: Historical Sources in Translation*, p. 279.

Page 94, line 24: *The Campaigns of Alexander*, p. 396.

Arrian. *The Campaigns of Alexander*. Translated by Aubrey de Sélincourt. Revised by J. R. Hamilton. New York: Dorset Press, 1971.

Bingham, Woodbridge, Hilary Conroy, and Frank W. Iklé. *A History of Asia*. Volume 1. Boston: Allyn and Bacon, 1974.

Boardman, John, Jasper Griffin, and Oswyn Murray. *The Oxford Illustrated History of Greece and the Hellenistic World*. Oxford: Oxford University Press, 1988.

Bosworth, A.B. *Conquest and Empire: The Reign of Alexander the Great*. Cambridge, England: Cambridge University Press, 1988.

Cartledge, Paul. *Alexander the Great: The Hunt for a New Past*. Woodstock, N.Y.: Overlook Press, 2004.

Doherty, P.C. *The Death of Alexander the Great: Who—or What—Killed the Young Conqueror of the Known World?* New York: Carroll & Graf Publishers, 2004.

Fine, John V.A. *The Ancient Greeks: A Critical History*. Cambridge, Mass.: Belknap Press of Harvard University Press, 1983.

Freeman, Charles. *The Greek Achievement: The Foundation of the Western World*. London: Penguin Books, 1999.

Hammond, N.G.L. *The Genius of Alexander the Great*. Chapel Hill, N.C.: University of North Carolina Press, 1997.

Heckel, Waldemar, and John Yardley. *Alexander the Great: Historical Sources in Translation*. Malden, Mass.: Blackwell Publishing, 2004.

Lonsdale, David J. *Alexander the Great, Killer of Men: History's Greatest Conqueror and the Macedonian Art of War*. New York: Carroll & Graf Publishers, 2004.

Perrottet, Tony. *The Naked Olympics: The True Story of the Ancient Games*. New York: Random House, 2004.

Plutarch. *The Age of Alexander: Nine Greek Lives*. Translated by Ian Scott-Kilvert. London: Penguin Books, 1973.

Rogers, Guy MacLean. *Alexander: The Ambiguity of Greatness*. New York: Random House, 2004.

Wood, Michael. *In the Footsteps of Alexander the Great: A Journey from Greece to Asia*. Berkeley: University of California Press, 1997.

Zimmerman, John Edward. *Dictionary of Classical Mythology*. New York: Harper & Row, 1964.

Michael Burgan is a freelance writer of books for children and adults. A history graduate of the University of Connecticut, he has written more than 90 fiction and nonfiction children's books. For adult audiences, he has written news articles, essays, and plays. Michael Burgan is a recipient of an Educational Press Association of America award.

Image Credits